What's For Pudding?

A comedy in one act

David Tristram

A SAMUEL FRENCH ACTING EDITION

SAMUEL
FRENCH
FOUNDED 1830

SAMUELFRENCH.COM
SAMUELFRENCH-LONDON.CO.UK

FOR PRODUCTION ENQUIRIES

UNITED STATES AND CANADA
Info@SamuelFrench.com
1-866-598-8449

UNITED KINGDOM AND EUROPE
Theatre@SamuelFrench-London.co.uk
020-7255-4302

Each title is subject to availability from Samuel French, depending upon country of performance. Please be aware that *WHAT'S FOR PUDDING?* may not be licensed by Samuel French in your territory. Professional and amateur producers should contact the nearest Samuel French office or licensing partner to verify availability.

MUSIC USE NOTE

Licensees are solely responsible for obtaining formal written permission from copyright owners to use copyrighted music in the performance of this play and are strongly cautioned to do so. If no such permission is obtained by the licensee, then the licensee must use only original music that the licensee owns and controls. Licensees are solely responsible and liable for all music clearances and shall indemnify the copyright owners of the play(s) and their licensing agent, Samuel French, against any costs, expenses, losses and liabilities arising from the use of music by licensees. Please contact the appropriate music licensing authority in your territory for the rights to any incidental music.

IMPORTANT BILLING AND CREDIT REQUIREMENTS

If you have obtained performance rights to this title, please refer to your licensing agreement for important billing and credit requirements.

CHARACTERS

Mary
Jack, her husband
Maureen
Ted
Dennis

The action takes place in a living-room

Time – the present

WHAT'S FOR PUDDING?

A living-room. It is evening

The set essentially contains a three-seater settee, two armchairs and a drinks table, but further dressing may be added at the director's discretion. There are two exits; one leading to the hall and the other to the kitchen

As the CURTAIN *rises, Mary is clearing up the remnants of a TV dinner, ramming the dirty plates onto a tray. Jack is sitting on the settee, fast asleep, with his mouth wide open. Mary gives him a disgusted look, picks up an unrecognisable leftover from the side of Jack's plate, and mischievously stuffs it into his mouth*

She exits into the kitchen, and there is an almighty crash of china heard off stage

The noise wakens Jack who, bemused to find his mouth full of food, starts chewing, and dozily reaches for a magazine

Mary enters, drops into the settee and sits moodily reading her book

Jack What's for pudding?
Mary What?
Jack What's for pudding?
Mary What do you mean, what's for pudding?
Jack It's a perfectly straightforward question. What's for pudding?
Mary Nothing.
Jack What do you mean—nothing?
Mary It's a perfectly straightforward answer. Nothing.
Jack I see. That time of the month again, is it?
Mary What—the time of the month when we don't have any puddings?
Jack You know perfectly well what time of the month I mean.
Mary Oh I see, you mean the time of the month when I'm menstruating.
Jack There's no need to be vulgar.
Mary Well actually no, that was last week. Not that you'd have noticed.
Jack And what's that supposed to mean?

Mary Because it didn't happen to coincide with your time of the month.

Jack You have to drag sex into this, don't you?

Mary Yes, I'm sorry, your Honour, it was a happy marriage, until I tried to drag sex into it.

Jack I don't know why I bother talking to you sometimes.

Mary I don't know why you bother either.

Jack What's got into you?

Mary I'm bored.

Jack What?

Mary I'm bored! I'm bloody bored! I'm bloody bloody bloody bored!

Jack All right, all right! These walls are only thin you know.

Mary Oh, that's right. Mustn't let the neighbours know I'm bored. (*She shouts to the wall*) I was just telling Jack how bored I am!

Jack Shhh!

Mary (*loudly to the wall*) Oh! Jack! Again! Hit me again! No, use the whip! Ahh!

In panic, Jack drags her away

Jack Shut up! Shut up! Jesus Christ, Mary—are you trying to make us the laughing stock of the whole street?

Mary giggles childishly

Are you drunk?

Mary No, Jack, I'm not drunk. I haven't been drunk for years. I can't remember the last time I was drunk.

Jack I can. It was Maureen and Ted's New Year's Eve party, the year before last. You threw up in the glove compartment on the way home.

Mary Oh yes, you made me clean it out the next day.

Jack Damn right I did. Bloody lucky my gloves weren't in there at the time.

Mary You know, Jack, you're the only person I know who keeps their gloves in the glove compartment. No-one ever keeps gloves in a glove compartment.

Jack And what precisely is one supposed to keep in a glove compartment. Shoes? Boomerangs? I'm sure they would have called it the boomerang compartment if that's what they'd in mind.

Mary Typical of you, that is. If someone says it's a glove compartment, you put gloves in it. That just about sums up your spirit of adventure.

Jack Well where exactly would you like me to put my gloves?

Mary Believe me, Jack, you don't want me to answer that.

The doorbell rings

Jack That's the doorbell.

Mary Well done. You've guessed this week's mystery sound.

Jack Shhh!

The doorbell rings again

There it is again. Are you expecting anyone?

Mary No.

Jack Who the hell could it be—it's after-half past nine!

Mary Perhaps it's the bogey man.

Jack Jehovah's Witnesses! (*He turns off the light and peers through the window*) There are two of them.

Mary Damn, you're outnumbered.

Jack Keep quiet. Hang on—it's Ted and Maureen! What are they doing here?

Mary Perhaps they've become Jehovah's Witnesses.

Jack exits to let them in. Murmured "hello's" off-stage

Ted, Maureen and Jack enter

Ted We've just had ours as well.

Jack What?

Ted Electricity bill—thought you were trying to save money.

Jack Oh, no—sorry. (*He switches the light on*)

Maureen Hello, Mary.

Mary Hi.

Maureen How's things?

Mary Oh, you know, never a dull moment.

Ted Guess what we've got!

Mary Venereal disease.

Ted What?

Jack Pay no attention to her, she's in one of her moods.

Ted (*holding up some tickets*) Oh, anyway, look.

Jack What are they?

Maureen Tickets for the dance up the club.

Mary Oh! When?

Ted Next Friday night.

Jack Friday? Bit short notice, isn't it?

Mary Oh Christ!

Maureen Is there a problem?

Mary Yes, I'm afraid we can't make it, Maureen. I've got to be in Bermuda by five, and Jack's flying over to the States to interview Michael Jackson.

Maureen Really?

Mary No, Maureen. That's next week. Actually, we've arranged to stay in on Friday.

Ted Stay in?

Mary Yes. We've been planning it for months, haven't we, Jack?

Jack Look, all right, all right. We'll come. There you go. (*He hands Ted some money, and takes two tickets*)

Ted Ta—only I thought I'd better let you know as soon as possible.

Jack You could have phoned—saved yourself a journey.

Ted Well, it's a nice evening—thought we'd take a stroll.

Jack You walked it?

Ted Yes.

Jack Oh. You haven't come in the car, then?

Ted No.

Jack Oh. Having a bit of trouble with the car, are you?

Ted No, no. Motor's running fine. Just thought we'd walk it.

Jack Oh.

Mary I'll explain it to him later, Ted. It's a tricky concept.

Jack You could have rung though, saved yourself the walk.

Mary Jack never answers the phone. I have to do it.

Maureen Don't you like the phone, Jack?

Mary He likes the phone all right. It's just when it starts to ring, it worries him. I have to answer it. In case it's bad news, or Jehovah's Witnesses have started telephone selling.

Maureen Oh, I don't like those Jehovah's Witnesses. Ted had a row with one once, didn't you, Ted?

Ted I did. I told him where to shove it.

Jack Shove what?

Ted His *Clocktower*, or *Watchtower*, or whatever the bloody thing was. I said to him—if God had meant us to sell magazines, he'd have . . . what was it I said to him, love? If God had . . .

Maureen If God had meant us to sell magazines, he'd have bought us all a newsagent's shop.

Ted That was it. If God had meant us to sell magazines, he'd have bought us all a newsagents.

Mary You always were one for deep theological argument, weren't you, Ted?

Jack Mary!

The doorbell rings

Who the hell's that now?

Mary It must be a Jehovah's Witness this time.

Jack looks through the window

Jack Oh, no. It's Dennis. What the hell does he want?

Mary What does he always want?

Ted Who's Dennis?

Mary exits to let Dennis in

Jack He's a complete pain in the ar——'d'you do, Dennis.

Dennis enters, followed by Mary

Dennis All right, Jack?

Jack Yes I'm all right, thank you, Dennis.

Dennis Mind if I have a quick look through your club book, Mary?

Mary Of course not, Dennis—have a seat. I'll go and get the club book, Jack, you introduce Dennis to Ted and Maureen.

Mary exits

Jack Right, er, Dennis, this is Ted and Maureen.

Ted Dennis.

Dennis Ted.

Maureen Dennis.

Dennis Maureen.

There's an uneasy silence. Ted stands, hand in pocket, rattling his change irritatingly. Maureen thumps him. He stops

Ted Well, I suppose we'd better be off. We'll see you Friday.

Mary enters, carrying club book, which she hands to Dennis

Mary Oh, come on, Ted, stay a bit longer—have a drink. We haven't seen you for ages.

Ted Well I don't know . . .

Mary Look, what's the matter with us all? It's Saturday night— we haven't got to get up for work in the morning. You're not driving, get a few down your neck! Let's live a little!

Ted What do you think, love?

Maureen Oh, I mustn't drink. I'm on a crash diet. Grapefruit and black coffee for breakfast. A glass of water and a digestive biscuit for lunch. And for dinner I'm allowed one egg and a bowl of roughage.

Mary Uggh! How long have you been on that diet?

Maureen (*checking her watch*) Forty-five minutes. Bugger it, I'll have a sherry.

Mary Great! A sherry for Maureen, Jack.

Jack Oh, right. What's yours, Ted?

Ted (*automatically*) Pint of mild with a splash please.

Jack What?

Ted Oh! Sorry—force of habit.

Mary Have a whiskey, Ted.

Ted Right.

Jack And can I get you something, dear? Hemlock, or . . .

Mary I'll have whiskey as well. A large one.

Jack (*cautioning*) Mary . . .

Mary It's all right, your gloves are safely locked away upstairs.

Ted What?

Mary Nothing. Oh, Dennis, would you like a drink?

Dennis Oh, no thanks, love, no. I won't be a minute. I'm only after a pair of trousers.

Mary Right. Come on, give me your coats.

Mary begins taking their overcoats

Jack Er, what shall I have?

Mary Oh, Jack, I love it when you're decisive.

Mary pops the coats outside the door and comes back

Jack (*at the drinks table, looking at a particular bottle*) Er, sherry, Maureen. Dry or sweet?
Maureen Oh, sweet please.
Jack I've only got dry.
Maureen Dry will be fine.
Jack Right. Ted?
Ted What?
Jack Dry or sweet?
Ted Whiskey.
Jack Sorry, sorry, yes, er, small one, or ...
Mary Just bring the bottle over.

Jack does so, but fails to bring any glasses. Mary impatiently grabs the bottle, goes to the drinks table, and pours out three very large glasses of whisky, forgetting the sherry for Maureen

Jack Right. Oh, sorry, Dennis, what was yours?
Dennis What?
Jack What are you having?
Dennis New pair of trousers.
Jack Sorry?
Mary Dennis doesn't want a drink.
Jack Oh, right.
Dennis Don't get me wrong—I like a drink.
Jack You would like a drink?
Dennis No, thanks.
Jack Right.
Mary Shut up, Jack. There you go.
Maureen Cheers.
Ted Good health.

They all take a swig. Jack joins in with the motions, but realizes he hasn't got a drink

You not having one, Jack?
Jack Yes, right.

Jack goes back to the table to pour himself one

So, what have you two been up to since we last saw you?
Ted Not a lot!

Mary, Jack and Maureen seem to find this slightly amusing, and emit a nervous laugh before falling silent

The budgie died.
Jack What?
Ted The budgie. It died. A few weeks ago.
Jack Oh, no. What a shame.
Ted Maureen was upset, weren't you, Maureen?
Maureen I was.
Jack Getting on a bit, was it?
Ted No, no—quite a young budgie really. Forty-eight, it was.
Mary That's really quite old for a budgie, Ted.
Ted No, I mean its human age was forty-eight, you have to multiply each budgie year by, what was it, love?
Maureen I can't remember now. Five was it? Or eight?
Jack I thought that was cats.
Mary How did it die?
Ted Maureen trod on it.

Mary tries to conceal an explosion of laughter, choking on her drink

Maureen I did not! It flew under my foot. I was cleaning out the cage with the vacuum cleaner. I always said Ted put that stand too high. I like to let him have a flutter around once a week, you see.
Mary Who, Ted?
Maureen No, Samson.
Ted That's the budgie. We called it Samson after her mother.
Maureen Shut up, Ted. Anyway, (*She demonstrates*) I reached up on my toes to hoover round the back of the stand, and when I came back down on my heels ... I heard a crunch.
Jack (*sympathetically*) Oh, no.

Mary cracks and is hysterical with laughter

It's not really very funny, Mary! I told you she was in a funny mood.
Mary Oh, I'm sorry, it's just the thought of ... oh dear. (*Still fighting back the laughter, she squashes her cheeks to resume a serious expression*) Did you bury it, Maureen?

Maureen No, that's the thing that upset me most of all. I bent down to have a look and it sucked up the hoover.

Mary wails with laughter, spraying her drink all over Jack

Jack Mary!

Jack struggles out into the kitchen to get a towel

Mary Sorry.

Ted It's all right. If you don't have pets yourself I suppose it's difficult to understand. To be honest I wasn't particularly keen on the thing myself.

Maureen Oh, Ted, what an awful thing to say!

Ted Well it's true. It was you who wanted the bloody thing in the first place. Kept saying you were bored at home by yourself.

Maureen I wanted somebody to talk to.

Mary Someone with the same interests as yourself, eh, Maureen?

Maureen How do you mean?

Mary Never mind, I think a budgie was a good choice.

Ted I wanted a dog.

Maureen Dogs are smelly.

Ted You can't tread on dogs.

Maureen Dogs can't talk.

Ted Neither could your bloody budgie.

Maureen Yes it could! It used to say all sorts of things! Ted even taught it to swear.

Mary I bet it swore when you trod on it, didn't it, Maureen?

At this point, Jack enters, drying his face with a towel, just in time for Ted to spray his drink over him

Jack Oh bloody hell! What am I around here? A bloody spitoon?

Ted Sorry, Jack. It's your wife. She cracks me up!

Dennis What do you think of them, Jack? (*He points to an item in the club book*)

Jack Eh? Oh, er, very nice, Dennis.

Dennis I like brown.

Mary Er, more whiskey, Ted?

Ted Why not? Better just make it a small one though—I'm walking.

They enjoy Ted's joke. Mary tops up the glasses. From now on, the drinks start flowing freely, and the tongues start loosening

Mary I haven't laughed like that since the night I threw up in Jack's glove compartment.

Ted Ha! When was that?

Mary New Year's Eve, on the way back from your house. Don't you remember, Ted? I got so drunk I started stripping off in the hall.

Jack Yes, well I don't think we want to be reminded of that appalling spectacle, thank you, Mary.

Mary Oh, charming. That's the way you view my naked body is it, Jack? As an appalling spectacle.

Jack Well, you're not exactly the trim young thing I married, are you, dear?

Mary Oh! It's all coming out now, isn't it?

Ted .That's what I said when I saw you in the hall. Ha!

Mary And what happened to the handsome young man I first married?

Maureen I didn't know you'd been married twice, Mary?

Jack No, she means me.

Maureen Oh.

Ted Well, time marches on for all of us.

Mary For Christ's sake, Ted. We're not that old. We just act it. None of us here has even reached forty.

Maureen (*thoughtfully*) Forty's quite old, really, isn't it?

Mary Maybe for a budgie, Maureen, but us human beings have a somewhat longer life span. Providing no-one treads on us.

Dennis I used to have a dog.

Mary What?

Dennis You were talking about dogs earlier, weren't you? I used to have a dog. Bull Terrier. (*This said, he goes back into the world of his club book*)

Ted Did you never have a pet, Jack?

Jack Yes. Well, it was Mary's really. Rover.

Maureen What sort of dog was it, Mary?

Mary It was a cat.

Jack Mary's idea of a joke. Poor little thing had an identity crisis. That's probably why it died so young. It was confused.

Mary Don't be pathetic, Jack. You can't die from confusion.

Jack Oh yes you can. I read it in the paper.

Mary Then why are you still alive, Jack?

Dennis Do they do these in brown, Mary?

Mary Those are slacks, Dennis—you need to look in the men's section—here.

Dennis Oh, right.

Jack Sorted your holidays out this year, Ted?

Ted Yeah, we've got a caravan for a week.

Jack Oh, lovely. Where is it?

Maureen Wales.

Jack Oh, nice part of the world, Wales.

Ted We don't like it particularly. We just go for the weather. Ha ha!

Dennis How much are these a week, Mary?

Mary Er, those . . . two pounds nineteen pence a week, over twelve weeks.

Dennis (*intake of breath to suggest too expensive*) Nice though.

Jack I know Wales quite well. Whereabouts is the caravan?

Ted In a field.

Maureen Don't be stupid, Ted.

Ted Well, I can't remember the bloody place. It's that ridiculous unpronounceable Welsh name. What is it, Maureen?

Maureen Rhyl.

Ted That's it—Rhyl. Rhyl. (*He repeats the word, trying to force a strange guttural pronunciation on to it*)

Dennis Couldn't I have them over thirty weeks?

Mary Thirty weeks? I don't think they'd even last thirty weeks, Dennis. You might as well rent your trousers.

Ted You buy all your clothes from the club book, do you, Dennis?

Dennis Oh yes. It's a good way of doing it, I think. I mean, there's no way you'd just walk into a shop and buy a jacket like this, is there?

Ted No. No way.

Dennis Whereas, with the club, I can splash out a bit, without burning a hole in my pocket, if you know what I mean.

Ted Yes.

Dennis Mind you—it's funny I should say that, 'cos I have burnt a hole in my pocket—with a cigarette, look. That's why I need a new pair of trousers.

Mary Well, you take your time, Dennis. Excuse me a moment. I'm going to the loo. You three carry on enjoying yourselves.

Jack You're not going to be sick, are you?

Mary As long as I can keep my mind off our marriage, Jack, I'll be all right.

Mary exits

Jack I must apologize for Mary. I don't know what's got into her.

Ted No need, Jack, she's just speaking her mind. I like women who speak their mind. It makes a change.

Maureen And I suppose that remark was aimed at me!

Ted No, no. You speak your mind as well, Maureen—it's just that nothing sensible ever tends to come out. Ha!

Maureen retaliates by tipping the entire contents of her drink in Ted's lap. Ted leaps up

Bloody hell! You silly cow!

Jack Oh, Maureen! Ted!

Ted These are clean on tonight. You silly cow. This will never come out!

Maureen Of course it will come out. It's me that does the washing, isn't it? What would you know about what comes out? You'll just ram them in a basket when you get home, and hey presto—next week they're clean again.

Jack Shall I get you a rag, Ted?

Ted I don't know about a rag—I need a new pair of bloody trousers.

Dennis Want to borrow the club book?

Ted No. You silly cow!

Jack Hey, come on, Ted, keep it down. These walls are only thin you know.

Ted Right, you! Coat! We're going home.

Maureen I was just beginning to enjoy myself.

Mary enters

Mary Oh, Ted, I am sorry. I wouldn't have hogged the toilet if I'd known you were that desperate.

Jack Er, he had an accident with his drink.

Mary Well, I didn't think it was the excitement of the dance next Friday night.

Ted We're going home.

Mary Don't be silly, Ted. There's a bit of a frost in the air. You might end up frozen to the zip. Come on, come with me.

Ted Where?

Mary Upstairs. I'll find you an old pair of Jack's you can wear till these have dried out.

Ted Well I . . .

Mary Come on, I won't bite you.

Mary leads Ted out

Jack Don't believe a word of it, Ted. She'll chew you to pieces. Another drink, Maureen?

Maureen Oh, go on then. I shouldn't really, it'll probably go straight to my head.

Jack Well, what the hell? The last one went straight to Ted's crutch—whiskey again?

Maureen No, sherry.

Jack Oh. I think we've been giving you whiskey.

Maureen Really? I thought it tasted a bit strong. I put it down to being dry. I don't usually have dry, you see.

Jack Well, you may as well stick to whiskey now. Better not mix your drinks. (*He hands her a large glass*) There you go.

Maureen Thanks.

Jack You're welcome.

Uneasy pause

Dennis I don't think you can beat Wales.

Maureen You go to Wales as well, do you, Dennis?

Dennis Every year—rain or shine. Mind you it's been bloody rain every year yet. Vera likes it though.

Maureen Whereabouts do you go, Dennis?

Dennis Oh, er, I'm like your Ted, I can't get my tongue round half the names up there. Name me one beginning with C.

Jack Cardiff.

Dennis That's the bugger!

Maureen Oh, Cardiff—did you go in the Castle?

Dennis No, we hired a log cabin for the week. (*He goes back to his book*)

Jack Are you happy, Maureen?

Maureen Quite merry, thank you.

Jack No, I mean, are you happy? You know—are you content?

Maureen With what?

Jack With your life. With Ted.

Maureen Which shall I answer first?

Jack We're not.

Maureen Who—you and Mary?

Jack Well, Mary. And me.

Maureen What's up?

Jack I don't know. I think she's bored.

Maureen Mary? Bored? How can she be bored, married to you?

Jack Well that's what I thought. (*He reflects*) Are you taking the piss?

Maureen No! I've always found you interesting, Jack.

Jack Really?

Maureen (*now beginning to slur her words*) Really. But then, I am married to Ted. Ted's about as interesting as . . . as a paper clip.

Jack I thought you and Ted always got on OK, as married couples go.

Maureen Huh! You don't see the half of it, Jack. He's a hell of a flirt, you know.

Jack Ted?

Maureen Thinks he's God's gift to women.

Jack Ted!?

Maureen I'm telling you, I wouldn't throw him as far as I could trust him. One glimpse of a woman's thigh, and he's up there like a rabbit down a drainpipe.

Jack Now I wouldn't have thought that of Ted. (*Thoughtfully*) They've been gone a long time.

Pause. Then they both leap up

Ted and Mary enter laughing, Ted wearing a pair of pyjama bottoms. Jack and Maureen both sit down again automatically

Mary Here's another one for you, Ted. What do you get if you cross an accountant with a gorilla?

Ted Give in.

Mary A backward gorilla!

They both enjoy the joke

And another, and another. What do you call an accountant with an IQ of three?

Ted I don't know. What do you call an accountant with an IQ of three?

Mary Above average.

Again they enjoy the joke

Jack This sudden surge of accountant jokes, Mary. They wouldn't be aimed at me, by any chance?

Mary You dear? Oh, I plain forgot—you're an accountant, aren't you!

Jack Yes dear, if you remember, it's the humble profession which has kept a roof over your head for the last fifteen years.

Mary Oh, I'm so sorry, dear, I forgot. When I walked in just now you exuded such charisma I thought for a moment you were a secret agent.

Jack Sorry to disappoint you, dear. You see, Maureen? Mary thinks I'm a boring fart, don't you, Mary?

Mary Well I don't know, Jack. That makes you sound too interesting. After all, farts can be fascinating things. Secretive, deadly, of unknown origin—no, you're just plain boring, Jack. You make Steve Davis look interesting.

Ted Now, come on you two ...

Jack You're deluding yourself, Mary. I'm as interesting as the next man.

Mary Well that's easy to say that when you're standing next to Dennis.

Dennis Sorry?

Mary Nothing, Dennis. Every time I suggest doing something interesting, he puts the blocks on it. It's too expensive, or it's not tax deductible.

Jack Like what?

Mary What about that balloon ride I wanted to go on last year?

Jack Ninety-five pounds for an hour!

Mary See what I mean?

Maureen It's a lot of money though, Mary.

Mary You know how much I wanted to go. It was a once-in-a-lifetime opportunity.

Ted They're not very safe those things you know. It could have just floated off into the Atlantic.

Jack I wish I'd let her go now.

Maureen I suppose they have to pay for all that gas.

Ted It's not gas, it's hot air.

Jack She could have just breathed into it.

Maureen Anyway, leave Jack alone. I think he's quite interesting.

Mary After the death of your budgie, Maureen, maybe you find a superficial interest in people like Jack. But believe me it will wear off. Jack is an accountant. He couldn't do anything interesting if his life depended on it.

Jack And what precisely would you have me do, dear? Scale a mountain? Declare war on Russia?

Mary Well that would be a start.

Jack Right! (*He suddenly takes off his trousers. He then proceeds to pour the entire contents of the whiskey bottle over his head, and leaps around like a demented gorilla*)

Mary What the hell are you doing?

Jack I'm being interesting.

Ted You're being a prat if you ask me, Jack.

Jack Well, I should consider joining me, if I were you, Ted.

Ted What do you mean?

Jack Well, Maureen said you were about as interesting as a pencil sharpener.

Maureen I did not! I said a paper clip. I never said you were as interesting as a pencil sharpener, Ted.

Mary No, well pencil sharpeners have got those interesting little bits on them, haven't they, Maureen?

Ted Get your coat you!!

Maureen exits and returns moments later with the coats

Jack continues to leap around, and Mary ignores him

Mary Have you found something you like yet, Dennis?

Dennis Well, I like these brown flares, but I'm not sure about the money. How do I stand, Mary?

Mary You've got another three weeks to go on the shirt, two weeks on the jacket, and one week on the shoes.

Dennis Oh, well I can settle up on the shoes now.

All this time, Jack has been leaping around like a deranged idiot. He stops, realizing that Mary is paying no attention

Jack I'm wasting my time here, aren't I? (*Now he loses his temper, for the first time*) I said I'm wasting my bloody time, aren't I, Mary?
Mary Quite frankly, Jack, you're a waste of everybody's time.

Jack grabs a small framed wedding photo from a table, and smashes it on to the floor. This sparks off an extremely fast, loud and angry exchange

How dare you!!
Jack How dare I what? Treat that picture like you've been treating me all weekend?
Mary My God! The worm turns!
Jack What the bloody hell is going on, Mary? Just tell me what I'm supposed to have done!
Mary You still haven't sussed it, have you, Jack?
Jack No, I haven't!
Mary All you can think is it's that time of the month again!
Jack All I know is you've been treating me like a dog ever since I got home on Friday night, and I've just about had enough!
Mary Perhaps it wouldn't have happened if you'd have taken me out somewhere special this weekend.
Jack Is that it? Is that what this is all about? You never said you wanted to go out!
Mary I shouldn't have to bloody say!
Jack I'm not bloody psychic! We never go out on bloody Saturday nights! You've never wanted to go out on bloody Saturdays.
Mary It's not the time of the bloody month, Jack—it's the time of the bloody year!
Jack What the bloody hell are you on about?
Mary Have I got to bloody spell it out for you, Jack?
Jack Yes, bloody please!!
Mary It's our bloody wedding anniversary!

Silence. Mary's anger turns to tears

Ted Looks like you're in the bloody doghouse, Jack.
Jack (*checking the date on his watch*) But . . . it's not till tomorrow.
Mary What difference does that make? You've forgotten, haven't

you, Jack? Like you always forget. Every bloody year. Not a present—not a mention—not even a bloody card.

Mary weeps uncontrollably, comforted by Maureen. Ted looks on in embarrassed silence

Jack goes outside the door for a second, and returns with a card

Jack Here.
Mary What's that?
Jack The card I've forgotten to buy you.

Mary wails, with a mixture of frustration and embarrassment

Go on—open it. You might as well, now. I was going to save it as a surprise—tomorrow morning. But ... well, that's a bit spoilt now, I suppose.

Mary opens it, reads it, thrusts it into Maureen's hand and turns her back in a final wail of anguish

Ted (*quietly*) What is it, Maureen?
Maureen (*reading the card*) "To Mary, all my love, Jack." (*She shows the card to Ted*) It's erm ... it's a ride in a hot air balloon.
Mary (*tearful, turning, and heading towards Jack*) Oh Jack!
Dennis How much do I owe on my socks then, Mary?
Mary Oh, fuck off, Dennis! Jack, I'm sorry. (*She hugs him*)
Jack Never mind.
Ted Look, we'll be off, Jack—see you Friday. Come on, Dennis.
Dennis Charming, I must say. If that's the way she treats all her customers ...
Maureen Oh, shut your face, Dennis. She's had a rough day.

Maureen, Ted and Dennis wander out
Mary hugs Jack, who accepts the affection rather uncomfortably

Jack Erm ... Is it all right—the balloon ride?

Mary nods, still unable to speak through her tears

Only, the man said, if for any reason you didn't want to go, I could have my ninety-five pounds back—no problem at all.
Mary (*backing away*) Jack, sometimes you really can be a prize tosser. (*She wrenches a smile*) But I suppose I love you all the same. (*She hugs him again*)

Jack Good. (*Pause*) So ... What's for pudding?

Lights fade to black-out

CURTAIN

FURNITURE AND PROPERTY LIST

On stage: Three-seater settee
Two armchairs. *On them:* book for **Mary**, magazine for **Jack**
Drinks table. *On it:* whisky bottle, sherry bottle, four glasses,
    wedding photo
On floor: dirty plates on a tray
Further stage dressing may be added at the director's discretion

Off stage: Club book (**Mary**)
Towel, anniversary card (**Jack**)

Personal: **Jack**: money
Ted: loose change, tickets

LIGHTING PLOT

Property fittings required: *nil*

Interior. The same scene throughout

To open: Interior lighting

Cue 1	**Jack** turns off the light *Snap off overhead light and dim covering lights*	(Page 3)
Cue 2	**Jack** switches the light back on *Snap on overhead light and revert to previous lighting state*	(Page 3)
Cue 3	**Jack:** 'What's for pudding?' *Fade to black-out*	(Page 19)

EFFECTS PLOT

Cue 1	**Mary** exits to the kitchen *Almighty crash of china*	(Page 1)
Cue 2	**Mary**: "... you don't want me to answer that." *Doorbell rings*	(Page 3)
Cue 3	**Jack**: "Shhh!" *Doorbell rings*	(Page 3)
Cue 4	**Jack**: "Mary!" *Doorbell rings*	(Page 5)